GREAT PETS

Ferrets

Johannah Haney

 **Marshall Cavendish**
Benchmark
New York

Marshall Cavendish Benchmark
99 White Plains Road
Tarrytown, New York 10591
www.marshallcavendish.us

Library of Congress Cataloging-in-Publication Data

Haney, Johannah.
Ferrets / by Johannah Haney.
p. cm. -- (Great pets)
Includes bibliographical references and index.
Summary: "Describes the characteristics and behavior of pet ferrets, also
discussing their physical appearance and place in history"--Provided by
publisher.
ISBN 978-0-7614-4153-3
1. Ferrets as pets--Juvenile literature. I. Title.
SF459.F47H368 2010
636.976'628--dc22
2009020561

Photo research by Candlepants Incorporated
Front cover: Juniors Bildarchiv / Alamy
The photographs in this book are used by permission and through the courtesy of:
Alamy: Jim Zuckerman, 4; Arco Images GmbH, 12, 36; neal and molly jansen, 16; picturesbyrob, 20; jack tait, 31, back
cover; Andrew Linscott, 39. Getty: Franco-Burgundian, 6; GK Hart / Vikki Hart, 8, 10, 23, 24; Gone Wild, 26. Peter
Arnold: Biosphoto / Klein, J.-L. & Hubert M.-L., 1, 13, 22, 25, 28, 30, 34. Wegner, P., 7, 21, 38; BIOS Gunther Michel,
15; Steimer, C. 18, 33; BIOS Decante Frederic, 40; Klein, 42.

Editor: Karen Ang
Publisher: Michelle Bisson
Art Director: Anahid Hamparian
Series Design by: Elynn Cohen

Printed in Malaysia
6 5 4 3 2 1

Contents

1

Furry Friends

A fuzzy ferret comes bounding out of its cage, shivering with excitement. He is ready to play. He leaps high into the air, then grabs its favorite toy and slinks into a corner to hide it. Running through a tunnel toy, he pops out the other end with a flash and zips back through for another turn. After a while, he gets tired and climbs into his hammock for a long, deep nap. The word ferret comes from the Latin word *furonem*, which means "thief." Ferrets are famous for stealing any item that is not too big or heavy for it to drag away into a secret spot.

Ferrets make great pets for people who want an intelligent furry friend.

Ferrets were first used to hunt rabbits and other small animals.

The scientific name for ferrets is *Mustela putorius furo.* Because ferrets belong to the Musteladae family, they are known as mustelids. Other mustelids include weasels, badgers, skunks, otters, minks, and polecats. People **domesticated** ferrets thousands of years ago. An animal that has been domesticated lives with humans and may help them fulfill some need. It is believed that people first domesticated ferrets so they could help humans catch rabbits and control mice. In some countries in Europe and in Australia, ferrets still help humans hunt rabbits by chasing them out into the open. In the United States, ferrets are mostly kept as pets.

Ferrets can be wonderful pets, but they are not necessarily right for every home.

Ferrets are active, joyful animals and popular pets. It can be a delight to keep a ferret—or even a few ferrets—as pets. They are enthusiastic players, and their long, slinky bodies make them interesting pets. Ferrets can be very entertaining little fuzzballs, but keeping a ferret as a pet is also a big responsibility. A ferret lives part of the time in a cage, but needs several hours each day of playtime outside the cage. One of the most famous characteristics

of ferrets is their tendency to steal away any item they can carry and hide it. Many ferret owners report finding their keys, cell phones, and just about anything else you can imagine hidden by their ferrets. Sometimes ferrets hide things in most unusual spots, like inside the lining of a sofa or box spring! This tendency of ferrets to hide things can be cute, but it also means you have to deal with losing important items sometimes. Also, ferrets must be supervised during their time outside the cage to make sure they are safe. Their cages and litter boxes must be kept clean. Ferrets also eat every few hours, which means you must give them fresh food and water often.

You might have heard people complain that ferrets smell bad. It is true that ferrets have their own unique odor. Ferrets belong to the same family as skunks, and they have scent glands that they use if they feel like they are in danger. However, many ferrets have these glands removed. Ferrets with the scent gland removed are known as descented. The oil that a ferret produces to keep its fur healthy also has a musky odor. Some people do not mind the odor at all. Others quickly become accustomed to it. Some ferrets do not smell as much as others.

The best way to know whether a ferret is the right pet for you is to find out as much as you can about how to care for ferrets. Head to a pet store to visit some ferrets before you make a decision. Ask people you know who have ferrets what the experience of ferret ownership is like. Once you are confident that you are ready for a ferret, prepare for many days of ferret fun!

2

The Right Ferret for You

One of the most important—and most fun— parts of having a pet is choosing which ferret to bring home. There are a lot of factors to consider, including where is the best place to buy a ferret, how to choose a ferret that is healthy, and how to find a ferret with a good personality.

One of the most common places to find a ferret is a pet store. Pet stores often have ferrets available at all times, and they should have a staff of knowledgeable people willing to answer any questions you may have about their ferrets, where they came from, how to care for them, and any special requirements. Sometimes ferrets sold at pet stores are already spayed or neutered and descented. Make sure the ferrets at a pet store have a clean

You must be comfortable with the idea of owning a small pet before buying a ferret.

Pet stores, breeders, and ferret rescue organizations have many different ferrets that need homes.

cage and fresh food and water. You want to look for signs that their animals are taken care of.

Breeders are people who raise a certain type of animal to sell to other people. Ferret breeders can be a wonderful place to get a new pet ferret.

Check the classified section of your local newspaper to find a ferret breeder near you. You can also look for breeders on the Internet. Sometimes breeders who specialize in ferrets can be more knowledgeable about ferrets than some employees at big pet stores that sell different types of pets. Like pet stores, breeders should keep their pets in a very clean environment, and should be able to answer any questions you might have about ferrets.

You should carefully examine the ferret and where it is kept before you adopt or buy it.

Sometimes a ferret owner can no longer take care of it, and must give it up. Other ferrets may start out sick and need to be nursed back to health before finding a family to live with. Rescue organizations can help these ferrets find a new place to call home. Sometimes rescue organizations will have baby ferrets, and others will be fully grown adults. Adult ferrets might be tamer than playful younger ones. Older ferrets also might be trained already, which can be an advantage. If you decide to get a ferret from a rescue organization or shelter, spend a little extra time with the ferret before making a commitment. Sometimes ferrets from other households have personality quirks that could be more difficult to change than in a young ferret, so you want to make sure you find a ferret whose personality matches yours.

When you are picking out your new pet, you want to find one that is healthy. Some ferrets may be sick or need medical attention that can cost a lot of money. Look for ferrets with clear, alert eyes. Healthy ferrets should not have runny mucus around their eyes, nose, or ears. The fur should be smooth and shiny without any bald patches.

When you are choosing a ferret, you want to find one that seems like it has a good personality. Ferrets can be funny little creatures, with a range of common behaviors that can seem confusing to people. One such behavior is shivering. When ferrets wake up from sleeping or are let out of their cage, they may begin to shake and tremble. But this does not mean ferrets are cold or scared. When a ferret is shivering, it is probably excited to start playing. You should notice that after a few minutes, ferrets stop shivering and continue to play busily. If a ferret is shivering at the pet store or breeder, it does not mean that ferret is afraid of you or fearful in general.

Young ferrets sometimes nip—lightly bite—people or other animals. It is important not to encourage this behavior so that your ferret does not think it is fun to bite. However, it is normal for **kits** to nip, and does not necessarily mean the ferret will grow up to be a mean adult.

Spend some time playing with different ferrets at the pet store, breeder, or rescue organization. Look for a ferret that seems to make a connection

Careful research will help you choose the ferret that is perfect for you.

with you. Finding the right ferret is the first important step in a life full of happy ferret fun.

Some areas of the United States are "ferret-free zones." This means that it is illegal to keep a ferret as a pet in these areas. Some people are concerned that ferrets are wild animals, that they might spread rabies, or that if a ferret escapes into the wild, it can pose a threat to the animals in the wild.

Be sure to hold and handle the ferret before you bring it home.

California, Hawaii, Washington, D.C., and some parts of Ohio, Minnesota, and Oklahoma all have laws preventing people from keeping pet ferrets. Other areas, such as Illinois, New Jersey, and Rhode Island, require a license to keep a ferret as a pet. Some of these licenses have a one-time or annual fee. Ferret lovers in many of these areas are working to change laws so that people are free to keep ferrets as pets. In the meantime, be careful to check with your local department of wildlife, humane society, or a local veterinarian to find out whether ferrets are legal where you live.

3

Types of Ferrets

There are two main types of ferrets in North America: the domesticated ferret and wild ferrets. Wild ferrets are known as the **black-footed ferrets**. These ferrets are endangered in North America, which means they are in danger of disappearing forever. Domesticated ferrets are related to black-footed ferrets, but they are different. The ferrets that people keep as pets are not the same as ferrets that are endangered in the wild.

Ferrets come in many different colors and fur types.

Ferret Colors

Ferrets are often identified and bred for their coloring. Certain people prefer certain patterns and hues in their ferrets' fur. The **undercoat** is made up of the softer, finer hairs closest to an animal's body that provide warmth and protection. **Guard hairs** are the coarser, outer hairs that protect an animal's undercoat. Some ferrets have a mask of coloring on their faces.

Having more than one ferret means more responsibility, but many ferret owners do not seem to mind.

Albino ferrets lack pigment. This makes their fur white, with ruby red eyes and a pink nose. Albinos are very popular among ferret owners. Unlike albinos of other animal species, albino ferrets are relatively easy to find.

Sable ferrets have guard hairs that are a rich, warm brown color. The undercoat can be white or cream-colored. Usually, sable ferrets have very dark brown or black eyes. A sable ferret's nose is brown and is sometimes speckled.

Be very careful when introducing your new ferret to other pets. Household pets do not always get along with each other.

Black ferrets have black guard hairs with a white undercoat. They have black eyes and a black nose, which is sometimes spotted or mottled. Black sable ferrets display a mix of black and sable characteristics. They have darker fur than sable ferrets, but lighter fur than black ferrets.

Champagne ferrets have a light tan plume of guard hairs with a white or golden-colored undercoat. Their eyes are darker than an albino's eyes—usually a deeper burgundy color.

Cinnamon ferrets have a warm, reddish-brown coat with a white or golden under-coat. Their eyes are burgundy.

Dark-eyed white ferrets are albino-look-alikes. However, they actually do not lack pigmentation like true albinos. Their fur is white or cream-colored, but their eyes are not ruby red like albinos'. Instead, dark-eyed whites have burgundy, brown, or

Ferrets are very popular because of their size and sweet personalities.

black eyes. These ferrets are also called black-eyed whites or dark-eyed white patterns.

Ferret Fur Patterns

Color is not the only characteristic that distinguishes different types of ferrets. The pattern of the fur is important, too. Just as a leopard has spots and zebras have stripes, ferrets have patterns in their fur also. But there are several different types of patterns in ferrets.

Ferrets with a solid pattern have guard hairs of the same color on their whole bodies. If it looks like your ferret is wearing white mittens, it is displaying the mitt pattern. **Mitts** can include white fur on a ferret's paws, as well as white knee patches, a white tip on the tail, or a bib, which is a white patch on a ferret's chest.

A roan pattern means a ferret's guard hairs are about half colored and

Some ferrets are light brown with more white around their heads.

An albino ferret has white fur and red eyes.

Most ferrets have dark bands, or a mask, around their eyes.

half white. For example, a sable roan ferret will have about half sable guard hairs and half white guard hairs.

Point ferrets—also known as Siamese—have darker legs and tails and lighter bodies. A ferret with a blaze pattern has a light-colored streak starting at the forehead and traveling between the ears and along the back as far as the shoulder blades.

The panda pattern means a ferret of any color has a white head and bib. Usually, ferrets with a panda pattern also have white mitts and sometimes knee patches and a white tip on the tail.

Some people enter their ferrets into shows, similar to dog shows, where ferrets are judged by how perfectly they display certain

Ferrets make great pets no matter what their color or fur is like.

characteristics. Ferret shows use the color and pattern combinations to find the best display of these characteristics.

No matter what color your ferret is, it needs a lot of love and attention. Knowing how to properly care for your ferret is the key to a happy ferret.

NICKNAMES AND TATTOOS

People who love ferrets have a few nicknames for their slinky friends. You might hear ferrets called carpet sharks, fuzzballs, ferts, fuzzies, or weasels. Males ferrets who are not neutered are called **hobs.** Neutered males are known as **gibs.** Unspayed females are called **jills,** and spayed females are called sprites. Baby ferrets are known as kits.

You might notice a small dot or two tattooed inside one or both of your ferret's ears. Many breeders mark their ferrets by tattooing a small dot in one ear. Sometimes there is one dot to indicate that ferret has been spayed or neutered, and one dot to indicate the ferret has been descented. If you notice tattoos in a ferret's ears, ask the breeder, pet store, shelter, or rescue organization what they mean.

4

Life with Your Ferret

Providing a home for a pet ferret is a big responsibility because ferrets need a lot of attention. They need a clean cage to sleep in, fresh food and water, toys to play with, occasional baths and nail trims, and visits to the veterinarian. Ferret lovers know that the effort needed to take good care of a ferret is well worth the joys of raising one.

Housing Your Ferret

Ferrets spend part of their time in a cage and part of their time outside the cage. Large, wire cages work well for ferrets. Cover the floor of the cage with linoleum tiles, old towels, or another soft surface so the wire does not hurt your ferret's paws. Do not use cedar chips or shavings in

With the proper supplies, hard work, and patience, you can have a happy and healthy pet ferret.

The ferret cage can have many different tubes and hiding places for your pet.

your ferret's cage. Cedar can make it hard for your ferret to breathe. Do not use a glass aquarium as a house for your ferret. There is not enough air, it is very difficult to keep clean, and only the largest aquariums would provide the amount of space required to keep a happy ferret.

A ferret's cage needs to have plenty of space, including an area for sleep, an area for a litter box, and an area for food and water.

Deep Sleepers

Ferrets can be quite deep sleepers, and can sleep for up to 20 hours each day. Do not worry if your ferret takes long naps and it is difficult to wake it up.

A ferret should have a bed or hammock where it can snuggle up and sleep.

Ferrets love sleeping in hammocks. Other soft bedding, like old towels or clothing, are also good for naps. Most ferret owners choose a washable material so it is easy to keep their fuzzies' sleeping area nice and clean.

Feeding Your Ferret

If ferrets seem like they are hungry all the time, it is because they are! When ferrets eat, the food passes through their digestive system in just about three hours. That means ferrets need to eat every few hours, too. Have food available to your ferret all the time. Usually ferrets will only eat what they need, so there is not a large risk of a ferret becoming overweight. If your ferret seems to be eating too much or not enough, ask a vet to take a look.

Ferrets are obligate carnivores, which means they must eat animal protein. Vegetables are not easily digested by ferrets. There are some ferret foods available made especially for ferrets. Other ferret owners feed a high-quality kitten food. Either is fine, but do not feed puppy food or dog food. Dog food does not contain certain nutrients that ferrets need to survive.

Like all animals, ferrets need constant access to plenty of fresh, clean water. Use a bowl with a solid base so your pet cannot accidentally—or playfully—tip the bowl over.

Training

It is possible to train your ferret to do certain things. Some people have successfully trained their ferrets to come when called, beg, roll over, and play dead, among other tricks. Find a good time for training sessions, such as after a ferret has been playing for a little while. Training sessions should not be longer than a few minutes at a time. Reward your ferret for doing what you want it to do by giving it a treat, such as a raisin. Do not punish your ferret if it does not understand right away. Training takes time and patience, but it can be a lot of fun.

If a ferret is nipping, try **scruffing** it—grasping it firmly but carefully by the back of its neck as a mother ferret would to her baby. Say "no" firmly, and

You can offer your ferret a variety of fresh fruits as treats.

33

Ferrets can be trained to use a litter box to go to the bathroom.

then place your ferret on the ground. There is a spray you can use on your hands that tastes bad to ferrets, which will discourage them from nipping at your skin.

You should never, ever physically punish a ferret. That means no hitting, flicking, bopping it on the nose, pinching, kicking, or spanking. To train your ferret to stop doing something bad, you can try scruffing it and telling it, "no," placing it in its cage for a few minutes, or simply refusing to play for a while. Giving a ferret a treat when it is behaving well will help your ferret learn how to act on its best behavior.

Grooming

Any ferret owner can tell you that fuzzies have their own special scent. Remember, ferrets are cousins of the skunk, and they have scent glands that give off a musky odor. Some people do not mind the ferret scent. With proper grooming you can keep your ferret clean.

Some ferret owners give their fuzzies a bath every month or so, while others think ferrets should only get a bath if they get very dirty. One thing is for sure: giving your ferret a bath too often actually makes it smell even stronger. When the oils are washed away, the glands work overtime to replace them. That can lead to an even stronger musky odor. If you bathe your ferret, use a mild shampoo, such as baby shampoo. Hold your ferret firmly but gently, wet the fur and lather up. Make sure you rinse the suds from your ferret's fur very thoroughly. The water should be warm, but not too hot. One good way to help your ferret dry off is to offer lots of towels for your fuzzy to burrow through.

Did you know ferrets can get hair balls—a mass of undigested hair— just like cats? Brushing your ferret every so often, especially in the spring and fall when ferrets shed, can help keep your house fur-free, and can also

Some ferrets will stay still for their baths, while others will try to get away. If you are uncomfortable bathing your ferret, be sure to have adult help or supervision.

prevent hair balls. You can also try feeding your ferret a gel every few weeks that helps prevent hair balls.

All ferrets should have their toenails trimmed. Ask your ferret's vet to demonstrate the proper method of trimming a ferret's toenails safely. Nails should be trimmed carefully because cutting too close can cause bleeding.

Ferrets also need to have their ears cleaned out periodically. Ferrets are prone to getting eat mites, which can lead to infection. Cleaning your ferret's ears will help prevent mites and other ear problems. Moisten a cotton swab with a small amount of baby oil or an ear cleansing solution designed for ferrets or kittens. Make sure the cotton swab is not saturated: a little bit will do. Hold your ferret by the scruff, or the back of the neck. Gently swab the ear, being careful not to place the cotton swab too far into the ear. Make sure you can always see the tip of the cotton swab: that way you know you are not going too deep. If you are unsure about the proper method of cleaning your ferret's ears, ask the veterinarian to demonstrate for you.

Playtime!

Ferrets have quite a bit of energy, and providing the appropriate toys can make play time even more exciting—not to mention safer. Ferrets love to tunnel through tubes, under blankets, and in pockets. Offer a variety of toys so that your ferret does not become bored. Balls with bells inside, cardboard tubes, boxes, hard plastic cat toys, and squeaky toys are all good ferret playthings.

Ferrets can be given some cat toys to keep them happy and occupied.

Some people use leashes or harnesses to walk their ferrets outdoors.

Ferrets can be mischievous little creatures. If there is something they are not supposed to get into, chances are that is the thing they are most interested in! When you allow your ferret out of its cage, make sure it is confined to one or two rooms that you have ferret-proofed. Make sure there are no holes

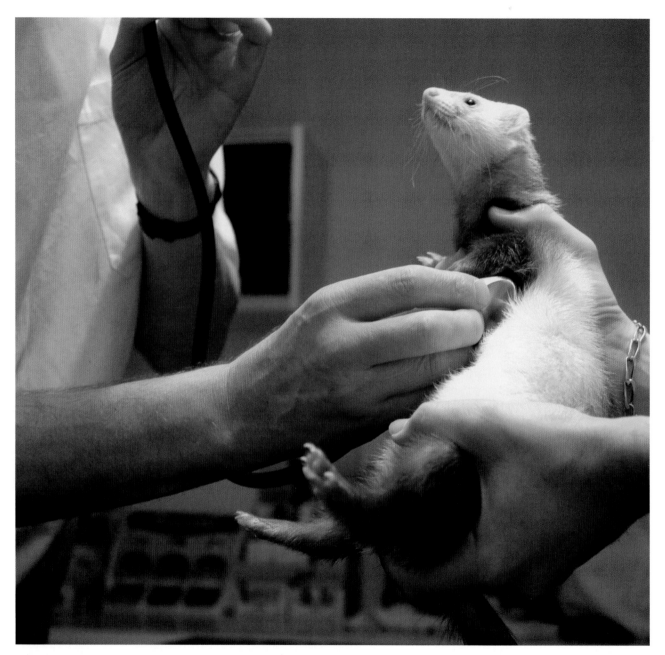

Regular vet visits are important for healthy ferrets.

in the floors or walls through which your ferret could escape. Ferrets can fit into tiny spaces—any space 2 inches or more should be sealed up. Make sure there is nothing valuable your ferret can steal and hide away. Keep wires and cords off the floor so your ferret cannot chew on them. If you have a reclining chair or a pull-out sofa, be very careful that your ferret does not get trapped when you open or close them. Many types of houseplants are unsafe for ferrets—besides, they would love to burrow in the dirt, making quite a messy game! Check piles of laundry and the empty washer and dryer for hiding ferrets before you wash your clothes. Ferrets will often run around underfoot, so be careful not to step or sit on your ferret. When you have guests, remind them to watch out for ferrets!

Vet Care

To keep a healthy, happy ferret, you must provide regular care from a veterinarian. When you first get your ferret, schedule a visit with a local vet. Your ferret's vet will make sure that the ferret is in good health overall. Ferrets are mammals, which means that they are capable of contracting and spreading rabies—a potentially fatal virus spread through saliva. One of the first things your ferret will need is a vaccination against rabies.

Pet ferrets should also be spayed or neutered early in life, which means that surgery must be performed to make the ferret unable to reproduce. One main reason for this is to prevent unwanted ferrets from being born without a good home to go to. For female ferrets, being spayed is a health concern.

Female ferrets who are not spayed and do not reproduce are at risk of developing a fatal illness.

Some ferret owners descent their ferrets. Descenting means removing the glands that produce a ferret's musky odor. Often, ferrets sold by pet stores are already spayed or neutered and descented.

Your ferret will need regular visits to the vet throughout its life to keep it healthy. If you notice signs of illness or if your ferret is injured you should make a special visit to the vet.

Ferret owners know that the work that goes into keeping a ferret happy and healthy is worth it. With the proper care, attention, and love, ferrets can live a long, healthy life.

A happy and healthy ferret can provide you with many years of fun companionship.

Glossary

black-footed ferret—A species of ferret that is endangered in North America. This is not the type of ferret that people keep as pets.

domesticated—An animal that lives with humans as pets or to help humans hunt or control pests.

gibs—Neutered male ferrets.

guard hairs—The coarser, outer hairs that protect an animal's undercoat.

hobs—Unneutered male ferrets.

jills—Unspayed female ferrets.

kits—Baby ferrets.

mitts—A fur pattern that can include white fur on a ferret's paws, white knee patches, a white tip on the tail, or a bib.

scruffing—Grasping a ferret by the back of its neck as a mother ferret would to her baby.

undercoat—The softer, finer hairs that provide warmth and protection.

Find Out More

Books

Doudna, Kelly. *Frisky Ferrets.* Edina, MN: Abdo Publications. 2007.

Feeney, Kathy. *First Facts: Caring for your Ferret.* Mankato, MN: Capstone Press. 2008.

McKimmey, Vickie. *Ferrets.* Neptune, NJ: TFH Publications. 2007.

Websites

American Ferret Association
http://www.ferret.org
This organization promotes safely keeping ferrets through education, shows, and ferret competitions. They also work to protect ferrets from anti-ferret laws and mistreatment. Their website offers information about ferrets, as well as a list of ferret shelters, veterinarians, and more.

Ferret Care Page

http://www.hsus.org/pets/pet_care/rabbit_horse_and_other_pet_care/how_to
_care_for_ferrets.html

This website offers great tips on how to keep a ferret as a pet, including
introducing new pets to each other, choosing a vet or pet-sitter, and tips
on travel and safety.

Ferret Central

http://www.ferretcentral.org/orgs.html

This is a listing of ferret shelters and organizations in different parts of the
United States and around the world. This is a good resource if you want to
adopt a ferret from a rescue shelter in your area.

Index

Page numbers for illustrations are in **bold.**

About the Author

Johannah Haney is a freelance writer, and has written several books for Marshall Cavendish Benchmark. She lives in Boston with her husband, Andrés, and their two pets.